Good
Character
Traits

I0171383

Positivity

Ashley Lee

Explore other books at:
WWW.ENGAGEBOOKS.COM

VANCOUVER, B.C.

𝑒 WWW.ENGAGEBOOKS.COM

Positivity: Good Character Traits
Lee, Ashley, 1995 –
Text © 2025 Engage Books
Design © 2025 Engage Books

Edited by: A.R. Roumanis
Design by: Mandy Christiansen

Text set in Myriad Pro Regular.
Chapter headings set in Anton.

FIRST EDITION / FIRST PRINTING

LIBRARY AND ARCHIVES CANADA CATALOGUING IN PUBLICATION

Title: Positivity / Ashley Lee.
Names: Lee, Ashley, author.
Description: Series statement: Good Character Traits

ISBN 978-1-77878-724-9 (hardcover)
ISBN 978-1-77878-730-0 (softcover)

This project has been made possible in part by the Government of Canada.

Canada

Positivity

Contents

What Is Positivity?

Positivity means **focusing** on good things even when it is hard.

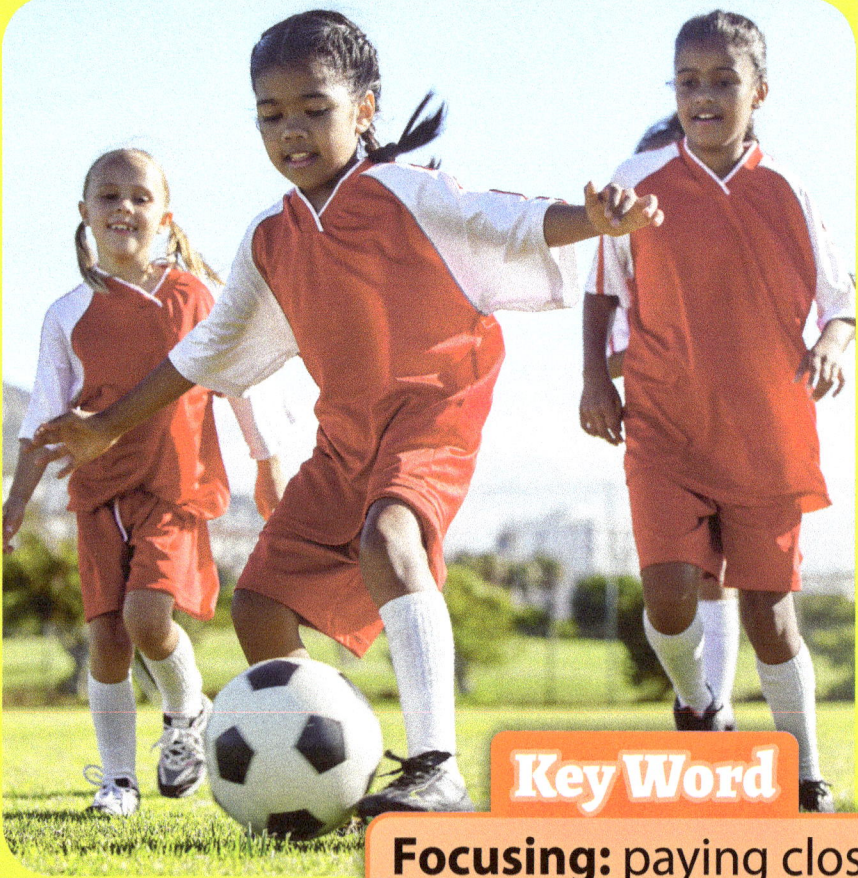

Key Word

Focusing: paying close attention to something.

Being positive does not mean you forget about the bad things.

Why Is Positivity Important?

Positivity helps people find happiness in small things.

Positive people are happier than others. They feel like their lives are important.

What Does Positivity Look Like?

Positive people see something good in everything.

Positive people are happy for others.

They are able to bounce back from bad things faster.

How Does Positivity Affect You?

Being positive can help you feel less **stressed**.

Key Word

Stressed: when people feel uncomfortable about something that is happening.

It may also help your body stay healthy.

How Does Positivity Affect Others?

Positive people are more likely to help others.

People become more positive when they are around positive people.

Is Everyone Positive?

Not everyone is positive. But everyone is able to be positive.

Some people are positive more often than others.

Is It Bad if You Are Not Positive?

It is not bad if you are not positive. Nobody is positive all the time.

Feeling sad is a normal part of life.

Positivity is about finding joy even during sad times.

Does Positivity Change Over Time?

Positivity goes up and down over time.

Happy times will make you more positive. But sad times will make you less positive.

Is It Hard to Be Positive?

It is hard to be positive when bad things happen.

But it becomes easier the more you **practice**.

Key Word

Practice: do something over and over again so you get better at it.

How Can You Learn to Be More Positive?

Try to find something positive about everything you do or see.

You might not like the rain, but it helps flowers grow."

Try not to **complain**. Say positive things instead.

Key Word

Complain: when someone talks a lot about how unhappy they are.

How Can You Help Others Be More Positive?

Give other people **compliments** when they do well.

Let other people know
you believe in them, even
if they are not doing well.

How to Be Positive Every Day

1. Make a list of things that make you happy.

2. Do not put yourself down.

3. Spend time in nature.

4. Exercise. It makes you feel happier.

Positivity Around the World

People all over the world **celebrate** different holidays like Christmas, Diwali, or Kwanzaa.

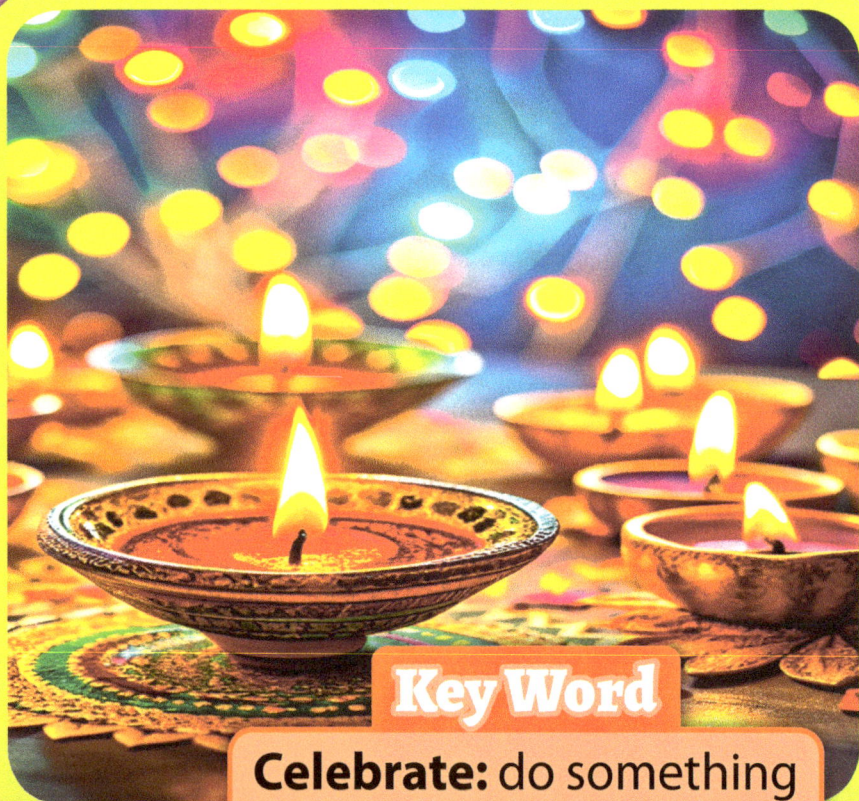

Key Word

Celebrate: do something fun for a special event.

These holidays bring people together and spread positivity.

Quiz

Test your knowledge of positivity by answering the following questions. The questions are based on what you have read in this book. The answers are listed on the bottom of the next page.

1 Does being positive mean you forget about the bad things?

2 Are positive people happy for others?

3 Do people become more positive when they are around positive people?

4 Is feeling sad a normal part of life?

5 Is it hard to be positive when bad things happen?

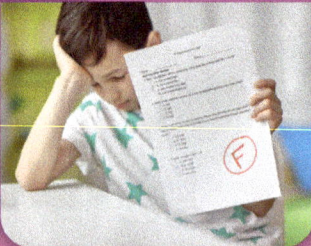

6 Do holidays bring people together and spread positivity?

Explore Other Level 1 Readers.

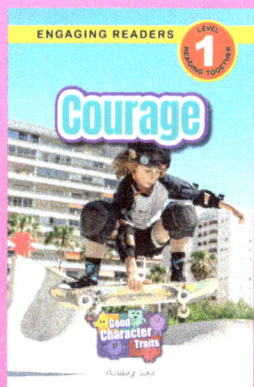
Courage

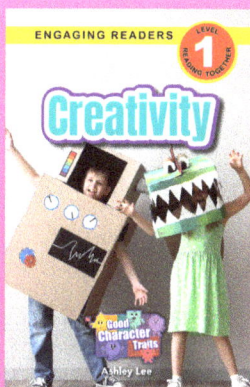
Creativity

Resilience

Respect

Self-Control

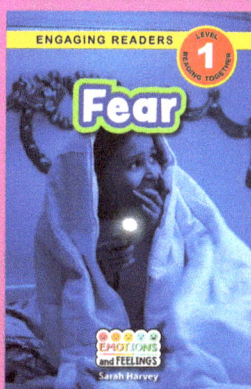
Fear

Happiness

Sadness

Surprise

Visit www.engagebooks.com/readers